The Rourke Guide to State S...

FLAGS

Jason Cooper

The Rourke Press, Inc.
Vero Beach, Florida 32964

ARTWORK:
Cover artwork by Jim Spence.
All flag art except for cover © The Flag Research Center.

EDITORIAL SERVICES:
Penworthy Learning Systems

Library of Congress Cataloging-in-Publication Data

Cooper, Jason, 1942 -
   Flags / Jason Cooper.
      p. cm. — (The Rourke guide to state symbols)
   Includes index.
   Summary: Describes the designs and symbolism of the flags that represent
the fifty states.
   ISBN 1-57103-193-6
   1. Flags—United States—States—Juvenile literature. [1. Flags—United
States—States.]
I. Title II. Series: Cooper, Jason, 1942 -   The Rourke guide to state symbols.
CR113.2.C66   1997
929.9'2'0973—dc21   97–20265
                                                                    CIP
                                                                    AC

Printed in the USA

TABLE OF CONTENTS

Introduction

States began to create distinctive flags for their armies during the Revolutionary War (1775-1783) and continued long afterwards. In Civil War days (1861-1865), armies still identified themselves by a variety of state flags. Later, with the growth of state capitals and national fairs, states began to sense the need for flags that could be used for non-military purposes. By 1901, 19 of the 45 states had official state flags. Twenty-five years later, all the states and two states-to-be—Alaska and Hawaii had flags.

Flags are strong symbols that can inspire people to laughter, tears, hatred, love, fear, and heroism. Each flag has its own personality and symbolism. None is without meaning.

In some state flags the symbolism is obvious. A picture of a miner, for example, makes quite clear that a state values its minerals. A few flags are cluttered with symbols and words—sometimes not in English. Some flags, though, show only stars, bars, patterns, or blocks of color.

State flag symbols have been passed down for a hundred years or more. Flags show life in the past; their symbols often reflect old battles and dusty days of rule under foreign flags. Instead of cars, computers, jets, rockets, and skyscrapers on state flags, you will see horses, cattle, plows, tall-masted ships, swords, and liberty caps that were worn as a sign of freedom. Four flags were inspired by the old Confederacy; several others were inspired by 18th century state seals. Looking at flags, you'll see a Milky Way of stars and an ark of animals—badgers to grizzlies to pelicans.

By today's standards, many state flags wallow too much in the past, or they are not politically correct. States have revised their flags over the decades for various reasons, though, and likely will change them again. Meanwhile, look at these colorful banners and "read" the fascinating stories they tell.

ALABAMA

"We Dare Defend Our Rights"

Statehood: 1819, 22nd
Year Made State Flag: 1895

Alabama's state flag is similar in design to the famous battle flag of the Confederacy. Alabama was one of 11 southern states that seceded from the Union and formed the Confederate States of America in 1861.

The most popular Confederate battle flag, the Stars and Bars, featured a blue cross, or saltire, against a red field. It had 13 white stars, one for each Confederate state government, arranged on the bars.

ALASKA

"North to the Future"

Statehood: 1959, 49th
Year Made State Flag: 1927

Alaska's state flag is a pattern of eight stars against a field of dark blue. The largest star, in the upper-right corner, represents the North Star and Alaska's title as the most northerly state. The other seven stars are laid out like the Big Dipper, part of the constellation known as Ursa Major, or Great Bear. The Great Bear is a symbol of Alaska's strength.

The blue field represents sea and sky and the forget-me-not, a wildflower that became the state flower.

A 13-year old Native American named Benny Benson designed the flag in 1926.

ARIZONA

"God Enriches"

Statehood: 1912, 48th
Year Made State Flag: 1917

Arizona's state flag, designed shortly before Arizona became a state, features a large, copper-colored star, standing for Arizona's copper and other mineral deposits. Thirteen red and yellow rays spread beyond the copper star, representing Arizona's sunshine and perhaps the 13 original states or the 13 counties in Arizona in 1911.

Red and yellow also recall the colors of Spain, which once governed the land that is now Arizona.

ARKANSAS

"The People Rule"

Statehood: 1836, 25th
Year Made State Flag: 1913

Arkansas is nicknamed the Diamond State for good reason. Diamonds have been sold in all of the states, but they have been mined only in Arkansas.

A diamond shape dominates the Arkansas state flag. Within the diamond, on a field of white, are four blue stars. The uppermost star remembers Arkansas as a member of the Confederacy (1861-1865). The other three stars in the diamond represent Spain, France, and the United States, the three nations whose flags have flown over Arkansas.

The 25 white stars in the blue border of the diamond represent Arkansas' admission as the 25th state in the Union.

CALIFORNIA
"Eureka (I Have Found It!)"

Statehood: 1850, 31st
Year Made State Flag: 1911

A grizzly bear appears on California's state flag. The animal represents strength and courage. The grizzly was wiped out of California in the 1920's, but like most flags, California's remembers the state's past. When the flag was designed in 1846, grizzlies—California's "golden bears"—were plentiful.

Early settlers wanted California to be independent of Mexico. To this day, that independence is represented by a star and the words "California Republic"—although California was never a republic, or independent nation.

Colorado

"Nothing Without Providence"

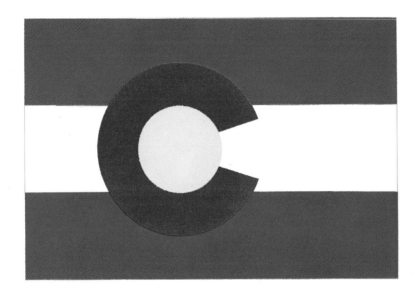

Statehood: 1876, 38th
Year Made State Flag: 1911

Colorado's colorful state flag has a large red "C" that represents the state's name and its admission to statehood in 1876, America's one hundredth birthday, or centennial.

The color red represents the meaning of the word Colorado in Spanish. The yellow circle inside the flag's "C" represents Colorado's gold ore and its sunshine.

The blue is for Colorado skies and one of the colors of Rocky Mountain columbine, the state flower. The white stripes represent another of the columbine colors, snow, and silver ore.

CONNECTICUT

"He Who Brought Us Over Will Sustain Us"

Statehood: 1788, 5th
Year Made State Flag: 1897

Like many state flags, Connecticut's has a field of blue. It's a striking background for the flag's white shield and three grapevines. The shield is similar to Connecticut's official state seal.

The grapevines represent the first Connecticut settlers, English colonists who planted the roots of their culture in what was then—the 1630's—a wooded wilderness.

The state motto, probably taken from the 80th Psalm of the Bible, appears in Latin.

DELAWARE

"Liberty and Independence"

Statehood: 1787, 1st
Year Made State Flag: 1913

Rather than the state's name, Delaware's flag shows a date: December 7, 1787. That's the day Delaware ratified, or approved, the Constitution of the United States and became the very first state.

The diamond design represents Delaware's rank as a political "jewel" in the late 1700's to both England and the American colonies.

The diamond and the figures in it are from Delaware's state seal. The farmer, ox, corn, and wheat represent Delaware's rich farms. The ship represents commerce at sea, and the soldier shows Delaware's readiness to defend itself.

FLORIDA

"In God We Trust"

Statehood: 1845, 27th
Year Made State Flag: 1899

12

(Florida continued)

Florida's state flag has a crimson X, or saltire, against a white field. The red bars honor Florida's participation in the Confederate States of America (1861-1865) during the Civil War.

The Florida flag displays the state seal in the center. Designed in 1868, the seal shows a Native American woman scattering flowers by blue waters. The seal also shows a palm tree, a steamship, and of course sunshine.

GEORGIA

"Wisdom, Justice, Moderation"

Statehood: 1788, 4th
Year Made State Flag: 1956

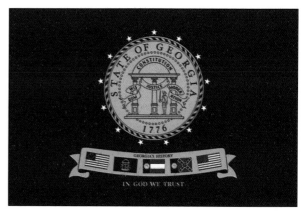

Georgia's red-white-and-blue state flag features the state seal and the old battle flag of the Confederacy. The Georgia state seal, changed little since its creation in 1799, shows three columns, representing the three branches of government: executive, judicial, and legislative. Ribbons with the state motto wrap the columns. A soldier, ready to defend the state's principles, stands by one column. The year 1776, beneath the columns, is the date of America's Declaration of Independence from England.

HAWAII

"The Life of the Land Is Perpetuated"

Statehood: 1959, 50th
Year Made State Flag: 1894

Hawaii's state flag resembles Great Britain's famous flag, the Union Jack. For much of the 19th century, Great Britain both protected and invaded Hawaii. British explorer George Vancouver gave the Hawaiian king, Kamehameha I, a British flag in 1793, and Hawaiians more or less adopted it as their own.

Today, the Union Jack appears on the upper-left corner of the flag. The remainder of the flag consists of three white, three red, and two blue stripes, representing the main islands of Hawaii—Hawaii, Oahu, Molokai, Maui, Lanai, Niihau, Kauai, and Kahoolawe.

IDAHO

"May It Be Forever"

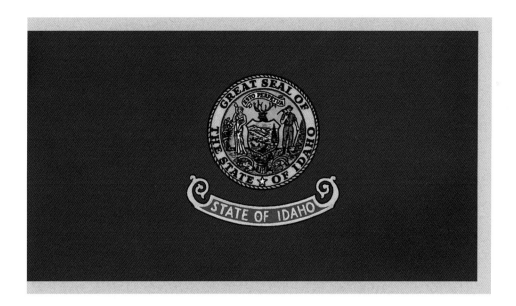

Statehood: 1890, 43rd
Year Made State Flag: 1907

Idaho's state flag shows the state's seal against a blue field bordered by gold on three sides. The name of the state appears on a gold-edged red scroll beneath the seal.

Designed in 1891, the state seal shows a miner, pick and shovel in hand and a woman. The miner represents the importance of Idaho's mineral wealth. The woman, accompanied by a liberty cap and the scales of justice shows liberty, justice, and equality.

The seal also shows rich farming with two cornucopias, or horns of plenty. The elk head reflects the state's wildlife. The state motto appears in Latin.

ILLINOIS

"State Sovereignty, National Union"

Statehood: 1818, 21st
Year Made State Flag: 1915

Illinois' state flag is dominated by a bald eagle clutching a red-white-and-blue shield. A boulder by the eagle's talons shows two years—1868 for the creation of the state seal and 1818 for Illinois' admission to the Union as the 21st state. Streamers in the eagle's bill show the state motto. The scene includes a rising sun and fertile ground.

Working in 1913, the designs used many features of the 1868 Illinois state seal.

INDIANA

"The Crossroads of America"

Statehood: 1816, 19th
Year Made State Flag: 1917

(Indiana continued)

Indiana's state flag shows a golden torch with seven rays and 19 gold stars against a field of blue. The torch and its rays represent freedom and the spreading of enlightenment or wisdom.

A large star above the torch represents Indiana. The remaining 18 stars symbolize the states that were part of the United States before Indiana's admission to the Union in 1816.

The designer won a contest sponsored by the Daughters of the American Revolution, an organization active in designing flags.

IOWA

"Our Liberties We Prize, and Our Rights We Will Maintain"

Statehood: 1846, 29th
Year Made State Flag: 1921

The red, white, and blue stripes of Iowa's state flag not only honor the United States flag, but also recall Iowa's association with France. France's tricolor flew over Iowa long before it became a state. Iowa became part of American territory when the United States bought it from France as part of the Louisiana Purchase in 1803.

The bald eagle in the center of Iowa's flag carries streamers with the state motto on them.

KANSAS

"To the Stars Through Difficulties"

Statehood: 1861, 34th
Year Made State Flag: 1927

The word "Kansas" appears in the state's flag in bold yellow letters. Above them, the state's seal and military crest appear against a field of blue.

The picture on the seal shows a colorful 19th century scene. A farmer plows with horses near a log home. Covered wagons move by, Native Americans ride after a herd of bison, and a boat steams upriver.

Three rows of 34 stars show Kansas as the 34th state. The state's motto appears in Latin above the stars.

The sunflower with a blue-and-gold bar is the state's military crest. The sunflower is also the state flower.

KENTUCKY

"United We Stand, Divided We Fall"

Statehood: 1792, 15th
Year Made State Flag: 1918

Kentucky is one of five states known as a commonwealth. "Commonwealth" appears on its flag, above the state seal and a wreath of goldenrod, the state flower.

Kentucky's seal shows two men greeting each other. One is dressed in frontier buckskin. The other wears formal dress of an earlier time. They represent a peaceful joining of different ways of life.

Kentucky's state motto, probably taken from a Revolutionary War song, is also part of the seal. America's Civil War tested this motto, as Kentuckians were divided in their loyalty to the North or South.

LOUISIANA

"Union, Justice, and Confidence"

Statehood: 1812, 18th
Year Made State Flag: 1912

Louisiana's state flag shows a pelican and three nesting chicks against a blue field. The state motto appears on a scroll beneath the birds.

Louisiana, the Pelican State, began using the web-footed bird as its symbol in the early 18th century. In those days people believed the pelican was a noble, self-giving bird that would tear open its own breast to feed its young if other food were not available. (In fact, pelican parents feed their babies partly digested fish.)

Besides giving the state its nickname and inspiring its flag, the pelican became Louisiana's state bird.

MAINE
"I Direct"

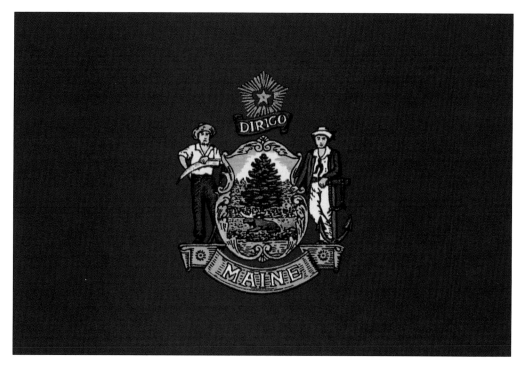

Statehood: 1820, 23rd
Year Made State Flag: 1909

Maine's Latin motto, *"Dirigo"* (" I Direct") refers to the North Star. it helped sailors find their way on the ocean long before modern navigation.

The North Star appears on Maine's state flag, as part of the state seal in the flag's center. When Maine was admitted to the Union in 1820, it was the northernmost state.

A tall white pine on the seal represents Maine's timber. A moose at the base of the tree stands for wildlife. Figures of a farmer and sailor show two important occupations of the 1800's.

MARYLAND

"Manly Deeds, Womanly Words"

Statehood: 1788, 7th
Year Made State Flag: 1904

Maryland's state flag is a tribute to tradition. It's much like the flags that Maryland flew in the 1630's, just after its founding.

Maryland's founder, the Calvert family, like other high-class British families, had its own coat of arms. Its black-and-gold coat of arms became the symbol of colonial Maryland and, later, part of the state's flag.

Black and gold show up also in the state bird (Baltimore oriole) and state flower (black-eyed Susan).

MASSACHUSETTS

"By the Sword We Seek Peace, but Peace Only Under Liberty"

Statehood: 1788, 6th
Year Made State Flag: 1971

(Massachusetts continued)

The Massachusetts state flag shows a Native American figure against a blue shield on a white field. A banner around the shield proclaims the state motto in Latin.

The Native American figure was borrowed from the first seal of colonial Massachusetts beginning in 1639.

The star on the shield represents Massachusetts. The arm and sword above the shield are from the state coat of arms, adopted in 1780. The sword reflects the state's motto.

MICHIGAN

"If You Seek a Pleasant Peninsula, Look Around"

Statehood: 1837, 26th
Year Made State Flag: 1911

Michigan's state flag features the state's coat of arms, a design dating to 1835. The elk and moose on the design may have been borrowed from Hudson's Bay Company, which ran the fur trade and English settlements in North America.

The figure of a man, one hand raised, the other on a rifle, represents a peace-loving state willing to defend itself.

On Michigan's flag, the U.S. is represented by an eagle and one of three Latin mottos, *E pluribus unum* (One Made Up of Many).

MINNESOTA

"The Star of the North"

Statehood: 1858, 32nd
Year Made State Flag: 1957

Minnesota's state flag presents the state's seal against a field of blue edged with gold. Dates in the seal remember the establishment of Fort Snelling, the state's first fur-trading post (1819); the year of statehood (1858); and the adoption of the first state flag (1893).

Minnesota's forest resources are represented by pine trees, an ox, and a stump.

The 19 stars on the flag show Minnesota's entry as the 19th state after the original 13. The French words *"L'Etoile du Nord,"* mean Star of the North—Minnesota's motto.

MISSISSIPPI

"By Valor and Arms"

Statehood: 1817, 20th
Year Made State Flag: 1894

Once a part of the Confederacy (1861-1865), Mississippi has kept the memory alive on its state flag. The old Confederacy's Stars and Bars occupies the upper-left corner of the state flag. Otherwise, the red, white, and blue stripes reflect the national colors of the United States.

The 13 stars of the Confederate battle flag symbolize the states that participated in the Confederacy, not the 13 original colonies or states.

MISSOURI

"Let the Welfare of the People Be the Supreme Law"

Statehood: 1821, 24th
Year Made State Flag:
  1913

Missouri's red-white-
and blue-striped flag
shows a version of the
state's seal in the center.
The circles of 24 white stars represents Missouri's admission
as the 24th state in the Union.

MONTANA

"Gold and Silver"

Statehood: 1889, 41st
Year Made State Flag:
  1905

(Montana continued)

Montana's state flag pictures the official seal against a blue field. "Montana" appears in gold capital letters across the top.

Montana's seal was created in 1864, when Montana was still a territory. The design shows mountain scenery typical of western Montana and the Great Falls of the Missouri River. The picture doesn't show pioneers, but it shows their implements—a plow, shovel, and pick. The Spanish words on a banner—*Oro y plata*—are the state motto—"Gold and Silver."

NEBRASKA

"Equality Before the Law"

Statehood: 1867, 37th
Year Made State Flag: 1925

Nebraska's flag shows its state seal of silver and gold against a field of blue. The state seal, adopted in 1867, is a glimpse of Nebraska in the 1860's.

The central figure in the seal is a blacksmith with a hammer and anvil. Nearby are sheaves of wheat and stalks of corn. A steamboat cruises the Missouri River and a distant steam train races toward the Rocky Mountains. The date on the seal, March 1, 1867, remembers Nebraska's admission to the Union.

NEVADA

"All for Our Country"

Statehood: 1864, 36th
Year Made State Flag: 1929

Nevada, admitted to the Union in 1864, late in the Civil War, put the words "Battle Born" on its state flag.

Below the golden scroll, a silver star and two stems of sagebrush form a half-wreath. Sagebrush, once important as medicine and food for cattle, is now Nevada's state flower.

The silver and gold colors on the flag represent these precious metals, both of which are found in Nevada. In fact, the United States Government hurried forward with Nevada's bid for statehood during the Civil War because it needed both metals for its war effort.

New Hampshire

"Live Free or Die"

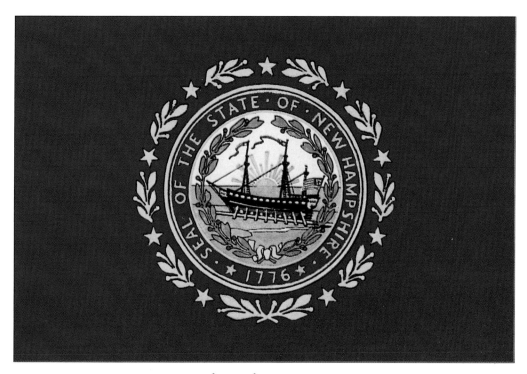

Statehood: 1788, 9th
Year Made State Flag: 1909

New Hampshire's flag pictures the state seal in the center against a blue field. The central figure is a tall-masted wooden ship. It is probably the frigate *Raleigh*, built in Portsmouth, New Hampshire, in 1776. The *Raleigh* was one of the first U.S. warships.

Green leaves of laurel surround the *Raleigh*, and golden laurel leaves form an outer wreath for the seal. Laurel is an ancient symbol for victory and honor.

The date 1776 is tribute to the signing of the Declaration of Independence.

NEW JERSEY

"Liberty and Prosperity"

Statehood: 1787, 3rd
Year Made State Flag: 1896

The buff-colored field of New Jersey's state flag is unique. Buff was the color that General Washington ordered for the trim on the blue uniforms of New Jersey soldiers and the color of the state's old military flag.

Much of the state seal, designed in 1777, appears on the center of the state flag. Figures of women symbolize liberty and prosperity. Liberty holds a liberty cap atop her staff, while prosperity holds a horn of plenty. Three plows also represent agriculture. Although New Jersey has the densest population of any state, it is known as the Garden State.

NEW MEXICO

"It Grows As It Goes"

Statehood: 1912, 47th
Year Made State Flag: 1925

New Mexico borrowed the sun symbol on its flag from the Zia, one of its Native American groups. The flag was sponsored by Daughters of the American Revolution and designed by an archaeologist and physician.

The sun symbol has many meanings for the Zia. For one, it represents perfect friendship among the united cultures.

The red and yellow in the flag are the colors of Spain. Spain ruled New Mexico from the early 1500's until 1821, when Mexico took over the territory that is now New Mexico.

NEW YORK
"Excelsior" (Ever Upward)

Statehood: 1788, 11th
Year Made State Flag:
1901

New York's state flag is one of the most colorful. It features the state's coat of arms, a shield supported by figures of Liberty and Justice, a crown at her feet. The crown stands for American independence from England, while the figures represent freedom and equality.

Other symbols on the flag include a bald eagle, the country's symbol and a globe showing North America and the Western Hemisphere. A rising sun and sailing ships likely stand for New York's Hudson River.

NORTH CAROLINA
"To Be Rather Than To Seem"

Statehood: 1789, 12th
Year Made State Flag: 1885

(North Carolina continued)

The North Carolina state flag has two broad horizontal stripes and a vertical stripe. The main features, however, are two dates on gold scroll: May 20, 1775, and April 12, 1776.

In May, 1775, citizens of Mecklenburg, North Carolina, may have issued a formal Declaration of Independence from England. But it is certainly true that in April, 1776, North Carolina's Provincial Congress voted to join delegates of the other colonies in declaring independence from England. This decision, reached at Halifax, North Carolina, became known as the Halifax Resolves.

NORTH DAKOTA

"Liberty and Union Now and Forever, One and Inseparable"

Statehood: 1889, 39th
Year Made State Flag: 1911

North Dakota's state flag is like the battle flag carried by men of the First North Dakota Volunteers during the Spanish-American War (1898-1899). The flag shows a bald eagle with a red-white-and-blue emblem on its breast. The eagle holds an olive branch, symbol of peace, and arrows, symbol of military might. The stars above the eagle represent the original 13 states. A banner proclaims *E Pluribus Unum"* ("One Made Up of Many") taken from the Great Seal of the United States.

OHIO

"With God, All Things Are Possible"

Statehood: 1803, 17th
Year Made State Flag: 1902

Ohio has the only swallon-tailed flag among the 50 states. Its designer likely took the forked tail from an old U. S. Cavalry flag.

Triangles formed by the flag's main lines represented the hills and valleys of Ohio. The stripes represented the roads and waterways. The white circle with its red center shows the first letter of Ohio and the round seed of the buckeye, Ohio's state tree. (Buckeye seeds are brown, however, not red.)

OKLAHOMA

"Labor Conquers All Things"

Statehood: 1907, 46th
Year Made State Flag: 1925

The shield at the center of Oklahoma's light blue flag is a battle shield of the Osage, one of several Native American groups that settled in Oklahoma. The blue color of the field is from the battle flag carried by Choctaw soldiers in the Civil War.

Two peace symbols decorate the shield: the calumet, or peace pipe (Native American), and olive branch (European). The designer wanted to show Oklahomans as "a united, peace-loving people."

Stars in the form of white crosses represent high ideals.

OREGON

"The Union"

Statehood: 1859, 33rd
Year Made State Flag: 1925

Oregon's state flag shows a large part of the state seal in gold. The heart-shaped seal, designed in 1857, shows a glimpse of Oregon at that time. A tall-masted ship sails in the distance. An ox-drawn covered wagon stands in the foreground. While the wagon symbolizes the settlement of Oregon, a plow and pickax symbolize two of the settlers' occupations—farming and mining. The ocean, mountains, and forests represent the state as a treasure chest of natural resources. A bald eagle, symbolic of the nation as a whole, perches above the shield.

PENNSYLVANIA

"Virtue, Liberty, Independence"

Statehood: 1787, 2nd
Year Made State Flag: 1907

(Pennsylvania continued)

Pennsylvania's flag shows the state's coat of arms. Two rearing black horses support a shield atop which a bald eagle is perched. The horses, each wearing a harness, represent the might with which Pennsylvania can escape difficulties and stay prosperous.

The shield pictures a sailing ship to represent trade, a plow to represent farming, and sheaves of wheat to represent the wealth of harvest.

Many elements of the flag's design date to the 1770's.

RHODE ISLAND
"Hope"

Statehood: 1790, 13th
Year Made State Flag: 1897

A golden anchor dominates Rhode Island's state flag as it did Rhode Island's first seal, designed in 1647. Later (1664), the word "hope" was added to the seal.

An anchor represents a foothold, firmness, and stability—what the Rhode Island colony may have meant to the first settlers. The word "hope" along with the anchor suggests a Bible verse— "...hope we have as anchor of the soul...." The seal may express the importance these colonists placed on freedom of worship.

SOUTH CAROLINA

"Prepared in Spirit and Resources"
and "While I Breathe, I Hope"

Statehood: 1788, 8th
Year Made State Flag: 1861

You would never guess that the symbols on South Carolina's state flag recall a Revolutionary War battle. Soldiers were aided by sabal palm trees, like the one on the flag.

Soldiers built a fort of palm logs to defend an island off South Carolina's coast against British attack. Instead of destroying the fort, British cannonballs sank into the spongy palms.

A crescent moon like that worn on the soldiers' caps also appears on South Carolina's state flag.

SOUTH DAKOTA

"Under God the People Rule"

Statehood: 1889, 40th
Year Made State Flag: 1963

(South Dakota continued)

The state seal in the center of the South Dakota state flag shows activities in the state when it joined the Union in 1889. A farmer, using a horse-drawn plow, turns over a field. A steamboat, representing trade and transportation, glides along the Missouri River. The state's Black Hills rise in the distance. Buildings represent mining and manufacturing. Cattle and corn represent the state's agriculture.

Rays of sun encircle the seal along with the name of the state and its nickname, the Mount Rushmore State. The state motto appears on a scroll within the seal.

TENNESSEE
"Agriculture and Commerce"

Statehood: 1796, 16th
Year Made State Flag: 1905

Tennessee has three geographical areas. The low country of the Mississippi River is in the west. Hill country lies in the middle. The east is a mountain realm. The state's flag designer honored the three regions with three white stars. He bound them in a blue circle to show that, though different in culture and landscape, they were inseparable parts of the whole.

The narrow vertical bar of blue on the flag was used, the designer said, "to relieve the sameness of the flag's red field."

TEXAS

"Friendship"

Statehood: 1845, 28th
Year Made State Flag: 1839

Various flags with one star have been flown over Texas since the early 1800's. A single white star has often been used as a symbol of independence, especially in the United States. American and Spanish settlers in Texas were involved in independence efforts against Spain and, later, Mexico.

Texas gained independence from Mexico in 1836 and hoisted a one-star flag. The new Republic of Texas replaced that flag with the present one-star flag in 1839. The Lone Star Flag continued to fly when the short-lived Republic of Texas became the 28th state in 1845. Today, Texas is the Lone Star State.

UTAH
"Industry"

Statehood: 1896, 45th
Year Made State Flag: 1913

Utah's state flag is a colorful blend of state and national symbols. The bald eagle and stars and stripes are clearly national symbols. The dates—1847 and 1896—and beehive are important to Utah.

A religious group called the Mormons settled around Salt Lake City in 1847. The group was influential in the growth of Utah and its admission to the Union in 1896.

The original name for the Mormon settlement was "Deseret," or "honeybee," from the group's *Book of Mormon.* The honeybee symbolizes hard work. The hive came to represent the state motto, "Industry", and Utah became the Beehive State.

VERMONT
"Freedom and Unity"

Statehood: 1791, 14th
Year Made State Flag: 1923

Vermont's flag shows much of the official state seal designed by Ira Allen, brother of the famous Ethan Allen, in 1779. The seal pictures a cow, wheat sheaves, mountains, and forest. A tall pine stands in the center of the shield. The head of a buck deer appears above the shield.

The symbols represent Vermont's farms and natural resources. Pine boughs are placed beneath the shield to remember the branches worn by Vermonters in the Battle of Plattsburgh during the War of 1812. The branches helped the soldiers hide from the British army.

VIRGINIA

"Thus Ever to Tyrants"

Statehood: 1788, 10th
Year Made State Flag: 1861

Virginia's state seal, adopted in 1776, is the centerpiece of the state flag. The state motto— *"Sic Semper Tyrannis"* ("Thus Ever to Tyrants")—appears on the seal beneath two human figures dressed as ancient warriors. The standing figure, Virtue, has her left foot on the chest of a fallen tyrant. His crown lies nearby. He has a broken chain in his left hand and a whip in his right.

Virginia's state flag has an unusual border of white fringe on the fly side; that is, the edge farthest from the flagpole.

WASHINGTON
"Al-Ki" (By and By)

Statehood: 1889, 42nd
Year Made State Flag: 1923

Washington's is the only state flag with a green field, representing the acres of evergreen forests in the state. It is also the only flag with a president's likeness. Named for the first president, the state honored the man on the state seal, which appears on the flag.

A jeweler in the state designed the seal—by accident. Refusing to engrave a complicated seal brought to him by a state committee, he drew a circle inside a larger circle, added a label ("The Seal of the State of Washington—1889"), and stuck a stamp bearing President Washington's picture in the center. The state committee approved the new design several weeks later!

WEST VIRGINIA

"Mountaineers Are Always Free"

Statehood: 1863, 35th
Year Made State Flag: 1929

West Virginia's flag shows the state's coat of arms against a white field with blue border. Rosebay rhododendron, the state flower, forms a wreath around a picture of two figures. One represents mining. The other represents farming. Two rifles and a liberty cap lie on the ground in front of the figures, symbolizing West Virginia's willingness to fight for freedom.

A rock between the men bears the date of West Virginia statehood, June 20, 1863. The state coat of arms was created that same year.

WISCONSIN

"Forward"

Statehood: 1848, 30th

Year Made State Flag: 1913

The badger became part of Wisconsin folklore because early miners in the state, like badgers, worked underground in hillside caves they had dug by hand. When the state coat of arms was adopted in 1857, a likeness of a badger was placed above the shield supported by a sailor and a miner. That coat of arms appears at the center of the Wisconsin state flag.

The flag's design is rich with symbols of old Wisconsin. A horn of plenty and plow represent farming. Mining is represented by a stack of lead bars, a miner, and a pickax. A sailor and an anchor represent the state's trade on the Great Lakes.

WYOMING

"Equal Rights"

Statehood: 1890, 44th
Year Made State Flag: 1917

The Great Seal of the State of Wyoming appears on the state flag as a giant brand on the shoulder of a white bison. The bison was an important source of food, clothing, shelter, and fuel for Native Americans and white settlers in Wyoming before statehood.

The woman in the seal represents the motto of the first state to grant women the rights to vote and hold public office. Men in the seal represent cattle ranching and mining. A bald eagle and shield show loyalty to the nation.

The red border is a symbol of Wyoming's Native Americans and the blood spilled during the days of its settlement.

INDEX

Note: States are listed in the order in which they joined the United States. Delaware was the first, Hawaii was the last.